T0064749

Bits
and
Pieces

David Hoye

WESTBOW
PRESS®
A DIVISION OF THOMAS NELSON
& ZONDERVAN

WestBow Press books may be ordered through booksellers or by contacting:

WestBow Press
A Division of Thomas Nelson & Zondervan
1663 Liberty Drive
Bloomington, IN 47403
www.westbowpress.com
1 (866) 928-1240

Interior Image Credit: Michelle Lees; Michael Lees

ISBN: 978-1-9736-9780-0 (sc)
ISBN: 978-1-9736-9779-4 (e)

Print information available on the last page.

WestBow Press rev. date: 8/18/2020

This book which combines poetry, prose and short verse
is designed to give my readers another side to my work.

Dedication

I'm dedicating this book to Betty Taylor, my mentor and friend, who has both influenced my poetry and given me the courage to try different styles of poetry. I 'd also like to thank the other Hartley Poetry Group regulars. Thank you all for your support.

I'd like to thank my wife Cheri, for her editing, and arranging both the poems and the pictures. Michelle and Michael Lees, Marcella Lees and my wife, Cheri, who provided the pictures for this book; I appreciate their contribution.

Chapter One

LITTLE BITS

Frustrated?

When will we learn that when we constantly bump our heads against a wall, our only reward is a severe head ache?

Success

The ladder of success leads continually upward; and men and women strive hard to reach the top, not realizing that once the top has been reached, there is only one way to go...

...down.

*****

If we spend as much time with our family as we do trying to make a success of our lives, think how successful we would really be.

Chasing Goals

Sometimes we are like a dog who chases his tail. We spend a great deal of time running around in circles chasing goals that always remain just beyond our reach.

Reality

Reality is where the dream ends and the day begins.

If only

If only I could try again
To look for that rainbow's end.
Just as it was then
When all of life was like pretend.

Giving

In our society a person is considered rich when he has a great deal of wealth and material things.

Yet, many of these people are still unhappy and often lead miserable lives. To me richness can be measured by what you give in your life, rather than by what you have gained. For it is in giving to others that you receive wealth that money never can buy.

Growing Older

Some people feel a birthday only represents growing a year older.

To me it means you have had the opportunity to live another year, and It gives you the chance to reflect on your goals for the coming year.

The Answer

I need to find the answer now
For I can no longer wait.
I will find it someway, somehow,
Before it becomes too late.

Changing of a Day

Today, it seemed so dark and cold,
And suddenly I felt weary and old.
But then I looked up and saw the bright sun,
And realized my day had just begun.

Happiness

Happiness can best be expressed by satisfaction with yourself and your life, but should never be mistaken for complacency. For the happy person is a doer while a complacent person is all done.

Enjoyment

Enjoyment of the simple things is the
surest cure for today's complexities.

Peace

Peace is knowing today is worth living,
and tomorrow will be provided for.

Beyond Ourselves

May we never become so overwhelmed with ourselves
That we fail to look for the needs of others.

*****

Do a kind thing for someone each day, and
God will prepare you for tomorrow.

Really Living

Let us always remember that those who never falter along
the way are those who never ventured beyond the doorway
of their lives?

Life

Now you've got it. Now you don't.
Maybe you'll hold it, maybe you won't.
I guess that's life, as they say,
You can only live it day by day

The Struggle

If only I could finally see
An end to all I know is wrong.
What a beautiful world this could be
Filled with a sweet bird's song.

Patience

Patience has never come easy for me
As I always strive for a chance to be free.
Free from restrictions to which I'm tied,
So that I may look to the other side

Try to Understand

Don't knock someone else
Until you understand
What makes them the way they are.

Actions Speak True

So many words we can say;
Words that can tell what we mean,
But I know there's a better way.
For by our actions, our feelings are seen.

Not So Long Ago

It wasn't so long ago
That I was lost and all alone.
How could I ever show
All the sorrow I have known?

Being Stronger

Tears are part of the life I know
Along with troubles they help me grow
Stronger and stronger each passing day
As I try to find my way.

I Feel Good

I feel good when I smile
Seeing that things in life are fine.
Then I find peace for at least a while,
Feeling so blessed by what is mine.

A Cluttered Mind

A thousand things are on my mind;
Things I cannot do.
How much easier would it be?
Were it only one or two.

Looking at others

I can look at others pain
And feel compassion from my heart.
For when our lives have seen some rain
We appreciate the sunshine when it comes again.

A Smile

One smile can have the power of a million words.

Sorry For Yourself?

Feeling sorry for one's self reminds
me of a Shakespearian play:
<u>Much to do about Nothing</u>.

Pain

It's funny how you never realize
how much pain you are in
Until it goes away.

Chapter Two

LIVING IN THE SPIRIT

Dreams

Dreams are nothing but pretty fantasies
Until faith and hard work help them to become realities

A Prayer Today

A Prayer today will keep tomorrow and yesterday away.

The Power of Faith

Counselors and therapists should
never forget the power of faith.
For even though it cannot easily
be transmitted to others,
It can, through example help to soften the fall,
in the battle of emotions in the rough road of life

Faith

Faith is the inner strength
that encourages you to fight for
what you believe in

Despair Brings Faith

Before we realize the true beauty of faith and living,
we must first have been through the depths of despair.

Faith of Youth

Hope may spring eternal in youth,
but where there is faith,
the spirit of youth need never fade away.

My Mistakes

Dear Lord, do not keep me from my mistakes,
But help me to have the wisdom to learn from them.

Death

Death is not an enemy, but rather an old friend
Who in the end, will come to visit each of us.

Habitual Grace

Christ supplies us with endless grace
Given, not earned, for you and me.
We need not win, nor fight, nor race,
Just open our hearts and let it be.

Psychology and Faith

As I delve into the intricate aspects of psychology,
let me always be aware that it is God who has
sent me on this journey, and everything I may
learn will be worthless unless it can be used
in serving Him through helping others.

Faith for Me

Faith has opened doors to a new and exciting life for me.
Let me always remember the darkness I once lived in
to appreciate the significance of my beliefs.

God's House

Church is not only a place to worship,
but it is indeed God's house.
Let us as members of His family
make His house our home.

Faith Fights Obstacles

At times in our lives we must face obstacles that seem
impossible to overcome, but our faith will help us
learn to cope with those things we cannot change.

Our Mission

God gives us a mission, may I have the faith and
strength to accomplish mine as He intends.

Things of the World

The world offers me many things,
My Lord shows me how to use them.

Wisdom with Faith

God gave me the ability to express
my thoughts in writing.
May he also give me
The wisdom to discriminate between thoughts
That should be expressed
And those that are better held within.

Faith Is

Faith is a sincere belief
That crops can grow
In a land where it seems
The wind will always blow.

If Only

If only I gave my heart to You,
I could save a lot of pain.
For You can show me what to do
All in life I have to gain.

I See the Light

Oh, Lord, I finally see the light
Shining through the clouds and rain.
Although it may not always be bright
It is enough to give us hope again.

Life

I ask not much nor do I expect
A monument in my name for people to erect.
For I'll not be famous or rich with gold,
But my heart will be happy and won't grow old.

For in my life I've always been blessed
With all I need to meet each test.
God has given me room to grow
Reminding me also to take things slow.

So, I've learned to see and hear
All around who need me near;
In my life I fully live,
But always have time to share and give.

As I Leave

I'm full of love and joy and grace.
As the Lord has blest me with needed rest;
And as I leave this quiet place
I'm ready once more to face life's test.

Living Our Beliefs

Faith is no more than living our beliefs
Even in moments when you're faced with grief
For it's in these times that you stand as one
It's important to realize that Thy will be done

Gift of Love

The gift of love is mine today,
God's blessed me with so many things
And every day as I pray
I thank Him for what he brings.

Life Without Hope

Life without hope is like a boat without a sail.
A heart without love is like a hammer without a nail.
Wealth without peace is like a crown without jewels.
Prayer without faith is like plumber without his tools.

Journey of Faith

The journey of faith is a different road for everyone.
Our experiences for each of us is second to none.
There's bends and pitfalls, smooth and rough,
Some difficulties are designed to make us tough.
Some of us are fortunate on our trips,
While others by danger are constantly ripped.
We go where God sends us, whether near or far
Although at times our life seems ajar.
When we look at the beauty and love all around
We know in our journey what we have found
It's His glory and wonder that always abounds.
It helps us remember our goals all around
To serve him forever without selfish gain
Knowing our journey is never in vain.

What to Do

I asked the Lord what to do
To help me learn to care.
He said to give with all my heart
The love which is mine to share.

So, now I go on my way
Giving all I have to give,
Serving You each and every day,
Showing others how to live.

I now know what You need
And expect me to do with your love.
Slowly and surely planting Your seed
Receiving Your help from above.

Don't Have the Time

"I just don't have the time."
Have you ever felt that way?
Like throwing a beggar one thin dime,
For I'm not sure that will change his day.

What if Christ felt that way too?
And he would hastily fail to see
That one thin dime just wouldn't do
Turning away to let us be.

But God's love for us is always true,
He is there ready to give
With many examples of what we should do
In giving to others as long as we live.

I Am Grateful

I am grateful.
Grateful for
For the love given me
Given me from your heart.
Your heart that full of kindness be;
Kindness be all that you know.
You know how much we can see;
We can see what comes from above.
From above is our God on high;
On high He see all we do.
All we do to show our love;
Our love that is given from only You.

Wishing on a Star

I always wish upon a star,
Seeking more than what is mine.
How is it I look so far?
Always seeking an important sign.
Yet, right here in front of me
Is all I'd ever really need
If only I will look and see,
Taking his hand and letting Him lead.
For my Lord is always there for me
He's the one who made the star
That I longingly wish upon.
It is He alone who can take me far
As I willingly wait for each dawn.

When I Look Around

When I look all around,
Joy and Love are often mine.
What we seek can be found
When we have God's guidance divine.

For with his love we can be
All the things that He needs today.
Opening our eyes so we can see
What can happen when we pray.

Your power is always on our side,
Keeping us safe all of the time,
Helping us comfort all those who cried,
Being there when the bell does finally chime.

Pain Helps Us See

Why does it take pain to help us see;
What's really important in our life?
Why must I be trapped before I'm free,
Struggling against heartache and strife.
The answers my friend, I may never know,
No matter what I may do.
But as I choose which way to go,
I'll ask for help from only You.
It is You who is with me now,
Showing me what I need,
Helping to give some way, somehow,
Knowing I need to learn how to lead.
For You my, Lord, continue to be
The only one I'll ever need.
So, as I walk and look and see,
You'll stay with me and help me succeed.

Giving Today

Thank you, Lord, for giving me today
The many blessings I do receive,
For each moment is treasured in a special way.
Through my life they interweave.

Each day you give to me
Is filled with love and so much joy,
Helping me live so happy and free
As with my faith I do employ.

For when we receive, we also must give
All that we get from You
As long as we each may live
Giving to others is what we must do.

When we know we've done your will
Delivering back all that we can share,
Receiving that wonderful and blessed thrill
Showing others how much you care.

God's Gift of Health

Little do we realize when we wake each morn
That we should thank God for another day:
With two strong eyes to see;
Two ears from which to hear;
Two strong legs to walk and run;
Two arms to lift and carry, and to hold and write;
For a healthy whole body, free from pain and illness;
A sharp mind which makes us capable of reason.
Let us get down on our knees and
thank God for our good health.
Then, let us go out and help someone
who is less fortunate than we.

I'll Never Be Alone

I'll never be alone
No matter how fearful life may be.
I don't have to do it on my own
Because my Lord will be with me.
No matter what tomorrow brings,
I have your strength and guidance, too,
Helping me know what needs to be done,
Keeping things safe for me and you.
For your love and grace have just begun
Keeping life much simpler for us all.
As all we need is to follow You,
Heeding your each and every call,
Accepting everything that You can do.

Why I Always Smile

You wonder why I often smile,
Seeming so happy every day.
My God is with me each coming mile,
Helping always to show me the way.

He is always by my side
As I walk along the way;
Always there to be my guide
Listening to what I have to say.

So, that is why I'm able to smile
No matter the challenge I must face,
Knowing that all the while
I am blessed with His grace.

Follow You

I know not where, or when, or how;
Yesterday, tomorrow or is it now?
I just know I must obey,
Following you along the way.

It's not for me to wonder why;
I must believe enough to try.
For only You know what's ahead,
Which way will I finally need to go instead.

So, I'm willing follow you to the end,
Turning each corner and around the bend;
Listening as I continue on
As You guide me to the coming dawn.

How Different Things are for me

How different things are for me
Since I let go of what I had become
Yet, I'm learning anew how to see,
Regaining feeling in what was numb.

For so long I thought I knew
What I needed in my life.
Instead of seeking guidance from You,
I only took my own advice.

But, now I know to come to You.
As I get down on my knees
Praying that I can see anew
The door You open and give me the keys.

My Budding Faith

My budding faith has brought me here
Teaching me the principles I hold dear.
Giving me the courage to find the way
Even when obstacles block the sun's ray.

For only now can I see
The beauty of life that waits for me.
For each new day allows me to care,
Showing kindness to others I can share.

My faith allows me to take the time
To be open and honest and make the bell chime.
Stopping at times to kneel and pray,
So, others can learn how their faith can stay.

On My Way

Lord, you've put me on my way
Where I'm going I do not know.
I hope I'll find the way to say,
To help my brother to live and grow.

If I need to give him praise
For how far he has come,
Or difficult questions do I raise
To make him look at where he's from.

He may want to stay where he has been
Going back to how things were.
That may not be where to begin
But I know he will not be sure.

Christis with Me

Christ is with me every day
No matter where, or why or when.
He always listens when I pray
Never asking where I've been.

For he knows what's in my heart,
Each and every feeling that's there
So, when I need some help to start
He will show me how to care.

As I walk, He's by my side
No matter where I choose to go.
Always with me as my guide
Jesus always loves me so.

A Time to Rest

Lord, let me listen to you
When You know I need some rest.
Yes, I can always find more to do
But that would not always be the best.

For at times I must think of me
As I kneel and say a prayer.
For then it is that You can help me see
That faith can help me anywhere.

So, when my rest is finally done,
Once more I can be on my way;
My strength and power come from the One
Who's with me each and every day.

The Resurrection and the Life

He is the resurrection and the life.
But what does that mean for me and you?
When we see only trouble and strife,
Can we really believe He set us free?

Yes, He died for you and for me, too,
Rising again as none before.
He clearly tells us what to do:
Follow Him forever more.

So, when we become overwhelmed with doubt,
Not knowing what it is that we should do.
We need to stand up and shout,
Knowing He will pull us through.

Sacrament of the Eucharist

"Come unto Me," says the Lord
As He gives his body and blood for you.
Celebrate this unearned reward
Christ lovingly gives us to renew.

He enters our life in a special way
Through body and blood we do receive.
Together joyfully He fills our day;
It's ours to share if we believe.

So now it's up to you and me
To choose His love and his care.
Do we have the faith that we can see
To take his love with us everywhere.

When we do, there is so much to give,
Sharing with all the friends we meet,
Helping them also learn how to live,
Showing His love ever so sweet.

Chapter Three

FAMILY

Family is family, whether you like it or not.

Life's Blessing

There is no greater blessing in life
Than to have a wonderful wife

We Do So Well

You and I do so well
On the way through life
It could be hard to tell
That we too know pain and strife
For we always try to smile
Looking towards the brighter side
We do enjoy our life style
Taking all our troubles in stride
We realize the value of each day
To always spend our time well
Thanking our Lord along the way
Enjoying life's story that we tell

Mother of the Bride

Mother's and weddings are quite a match;
It can almost send her to the looney hatch.
Tears and joy, happy and sad,
She feels all these things, good and bad.
Wanting terribly to stand and be brave
While trying hard not to rant and rave.
To mothers, it means her daughter she'll lose
Gaining a son that she didn't choose.
In these hectic weeks she'll lose her pride
But if she can make it, so can the bride.

Mothers-In-Law

The mother-in-law has a difficult task.
She must give up her children
While her feelings are masked.
She's given them love and all her devotion;
Yet, how quickly they're gone
Like fish in the ocean.
She fears for their safety, their care and their feelings.
Yet, pangs of loneliness send her mind reeling.
She has to adjust to her children's new mate
And be resigned to accept their fate.
Then, learn to love their new relations
And help them grow on strong foundations.

Being a Family

Being a family feels so good to me
Sharing love every day
Helping one another to see
Joining together as we pray

A Family

A family offers a wonderful gift,
of friendship and hope that gives us a lift.
We share our love, our pain and our grief,
Always together, we share our belief.

To Be a Family

We are a family joined with love
We fit together like a hand in a glove
Though we each are different in many ways
We join together in work and in play
Every day is filled with giving
As our family enjoys our daily living

The Gift

A little child given to me;
It was a most wonderful gift.
Beautiful and caring for all to see;
Her smiling face would surely lift.

All of the time of feeling down,
Thinking of only what goes wrong.
Suddenly vanish with our frown
Not even taking very long.

For the smile of a child can change our day
Giving us reason to see
All the gifts that come our way
The peace and joy that makes us free.

My Sweethearts

My sweethearts number not one but three
Each one means something special to me
The tenderness of my loving wife
That's given only once in life
The beauty of my first little girl
With a face aglow and hair full of curls
And who could forget daughter number two
Whose fresh view of life is like the morning dew
Yes, Lord you've made me the happy one
With three hearts to share under your bright sun

Mothers

What is a mother we all may ask?
What is behind that smiling mask?
For how could she really be
As happy as she seems to me.

What is it she really feels
With her children always at her heels?
What is that? You say she cares
Even with them in her hair.

You say she feels just love and joy
Even when she's stepped on a toy?
You'd think a mother must be tough,
For she has to be made of some pretty stern stuff.

Yet you say she's always gentle and kind
Always having her family in her mind.
If this is true then I must say
Every day should be Mother's Day.

Daughters

My little girls, oh what a joy,
Who says a man needs a boy
For little girls are such gentle things
Much like a cyclone in the spring
Everyone knows that girls stay clean
Never dreaming of being mean
So who's tracking mud on the rug
Giving the dog's ear a mighty tug
But little girls are still full of love
But it's not sugar and spice that they are made of

Our Child

When God gave us our child, we received quite a scare
We reached deep inside, as we shared a prayer
When her health returned, and we felt a reprieve
We knew miracles came to those who believed
Now, every day that she lives
We can experience the love that God gives
For as she breathes and walks and grows
We experience faith that only He knows
For each day with us is a gift from above
With our child, that gift is love

My Littlest One

My little one has a certain way
Of bringing excitement into each day
You never know what sudden discovery
Can bring her to some miraculous recovery
For she can change from being meek and quiet
To suddenly sounding like she's creating a riot
Her moods are not masked and cannot be hid
Often exploding like a kettle's lid
But she can give us endless joy
As we watch her learning to play with a toy

My Oldest Daughter

My oldest daughter, what a joy when born
She quickly became a little girl with curls to adorn
Now at age five what a joy to behold
Her love for life makes her so bold
Life is so simple but ever so sweet
Problems, like people are so easy to meet
If pleasure were ever meant to be mine
The world I live in to be fruitful and fine
These prayers were answered from heaven above
When God gave me my daughter, and a whole lot of love

On Being Three

Another year has come and gone
As if the sunset turned right to dawn
My daughter has made it through
That long and frustrating year of two

Now, at three, she's bright and gay
Knowing she's come a very long way
She's no longer our baby girl
As she excitedly gives life a whirl

I'm happy yet sad, to see her change
She's no longer our baby and that seems strange
But the love she gives can leave us no sorrow
As she boldly leaps toward tomorrow

My Little Girls

My little girls are precious to me,
Our time together helps to see.
Their growth and learning so many things,
Their presence, makes my heart sing.

Little Hands

Little hands reach out for me
Longing for comfort with a knowing plea.
She needs the love that I supply;
Needing to hear my warm reply.
For in her world I stand alone
Feeling like a king upon his throne.

My Little Girls

Doggie ears, and ponytails
My little girls so pretty and gay
Their constant laughter never fails
To brighten up a gloomy day

The Yellow Car

To me a car is just a car;
That and some gas can take you far.
Some are big and others are small,
But mostly, I've learned to accept them all.

But to my little girl there's only one
Which is as important as the sun.

For wherever we go in her yellow car,
We better make sure she knows where we are.
To her, there will never be a more brilliant star
That could ever compare to her yellow car.

Mom

My mom will always be someone special to me
For through the years she was always there
When I was a toddler and always in her hair
She loved me anyway and showed me she cared
Throughout all of my growing years
When I was in trouble, she was there on the double
No one could mention all of her duties
From cook, to maid, to nurse, to protector and teacher
Each day we expected her near enough to reach her
She was always cheerful and sweet and pleasant
Expected to look beautiful and resplendent
Someday I'll be able to tell her in some way
That every day should be Mother's day

My Dad

To me my dad was many things
Sweet moments of the past my memory brings
From the time I was old enough to reason
Dad was there whatever the season
To teach me to fish, to hunt, and to hike
He taught me to ride my very first bike
As I grew older and began to rebel
Dad was there when into trouble I fell
At times our feelings kept us apart
But my beliefs and morals came from his heart
My style of life may have had different ends
But it reflects his teaching and the example he did lend

Dad's Death

If only death would finally arrive
To take him to his final peace.
So, rather than just survive,
He could find that great release.

The End is Near

Finally your end is drawing near
The journey of life is almost over
Although the thought brings me fear
I know your pain would be no more
For life has been good to you
We have had the time to give
Having a chance to share our love
As a family we did live
With many blessings from above
I'll miss you and I'll certainly grieve
Feeling the loss of a life time of love
Yet, I know for sure as you leave
I'll join you again in heaven above

Brother Jim

Only my brother could know me so well
Through the years it's been easy to tell
Whenever I needed a little support
He was always there with a witty retort
He always was my biggest fan
Building me up as only he can
Now, I'm finally on my own
I'll always be grateful for the love he's shown

My Brother Jim

I am my brother's keeper
That's what the scripture say
Only now do I realize
That day has come my way

We really never spent much time
For he was so much smarter than me
It was more than just his rhyme
His heart was hard for me to see

But now we are together again
Age and illness have melted his soul
Now, helping him is as a friend
He's still my brother in a different role

Isn't it funny what time can do?
It takes away our foolish pride
Now, I'm feeling much closer to you
Because my Lord is still my guide

My Changing Family

Lord, it seems like yesterday
Both my daughters were oh so young
As our family shared in a special way
I remember the laughter and the songs we sung

But, now they're grown and on their own
Like beautiful young birds who have left their nest
They are full of love and their confidence has shown
They can handle many a test

For both have made their choices well
And for that we brim with pride
For as their parents our hearts do swell
Gently, with love, we still do guide

Grandparents

They have finally made a special day
Giving us all a chance to say
Grandparents are special and stand apart
For when they act it's from the heart.

Children of their own they did raise,
They certainly do deserve some praise.
But giving for them is never done
Their love is as steady as the rising sun.

Every day given them shows the way
To be with their grandkids as they play.
At times to heal their hearts and soul,
Grandparents can also play that role.

For all these kids are so special and kind
It's so great that they are yours and mine
Through our relationship we will find
Something that will always be fine

Grandmothers

Grandmothers are always full of joy.
Waiting there to share
Sometimes candy or maybe a toy,
Always being very fair.
But more than that they give their love
In a very special way.
For their gift is from above;
They give it every day.

Grammas

Grammas have that special knack
Of giving love away
They always wear that special smile
Knowing just what to say

Grammas always do what is right
They always seem to know what's best
Something always lets Gramma know
Even more than all the rest

Wisdom, kindness, and humor too
All are Gramma's own
For all over this great big world
Gramma's love is known

Special Blend

Grandmas'are that special blend
Of wisdom and of love
They're filled with kindness and care
As if straight from heaven above

They give to others all day long
They never seem to tire
No-one who really knows them well
Ever doubts their desire

For grandkids are their special joy
And fill up many an hour
While they help to mold them well
Like a bud into a flower

South Dakota Grandma

Both of our parents lived far away
Much too far to see every day
So our little girls were bound to be
Without a grandma to come and see

But we were lucky, for we had a friend
Who believed our girls should not pretend
For she was willing and able to share
Love and kindness with a Grandma's care

And she was happy to be a part
Being able to give right from her heart
She was our South Dakota Grandma, and we were glad
For she kept our girls from being sad

Grandchildren

Six grand-kids, oh what a joy!
Four girls and also two boys.
Each one special and apart,
Always able to touch my heart.

Grandkids

One of the joys of growing old
Is watching your kids as they have grown
They have become so confident and bold
Now, they have children of their own

Having grandkids is a great delight
From their birth watching them grow
Seeing your kids are doing it right
Is so comforting for us to know

Spending time with each one
Maybe even spoiling them a little bit
Gives us joy second to none
Each one is a special fit

Giving our love and caring too
Sharing time that is so fine
Letting them know me and you
It all part of God's design

My Grandkids

After a lifetime of parenting
How wonderful it is to watch my kids raise their own
To be a grandparent helps you enjoy
the joys of watching them grow
Without being responsible for their day by day care

Grandkids

Dance
Tae Kwon Do
Cross-country
School paper
Prom
All State Choir
Gymnastics
Wrestling
Barbies
Free-throw contest
Softball
Track
These are some of the things
that make my grandkids who they are

Chapter Four

PETS ARE FAMILY, TOO

My Rocket

A horse is a strange and beautiful creature
With a pride and stature that magnifies each feature;

Wild and free is their claim to life,
Stunning to watch through storms and strife.

Yet, that same horse is gentle and tame
When I stop and call her name.

That powerful, strong, and muscular frame
Is willing to bend and bow to my claim.

When I ride her and feel her power,
Me and Rocket in our finest hour.

Rocket

Young and wild she came to me,
A three year old filly full of fun.
It didn't take long to see
This wonderful horse was the one.

Her eyes were bright and full of fire.
She was a curious as she could be.
At times she would raise my ire.
Rocket's spirit was always free.

When I climbed on her back
Her sense of power came flowing through
Letting me forget the skills I lack
Knowing together all the things we could do.

She was a horse but so much more.
No-one knew me better, nor understood
My feelings touched her to the core.
Rocket responded as only she could.

At times when I needed to talk
She'd whinny and nod as if she knew.
Taking her out for a run or walk
Was all I needed to help me through.

Strong and beautiful, what a sight to see;
Proud and somewhat arrogant, too.
Rocket meant so much to me
As only she was able to do.

My Dogs

I've always had a dog of my own,
Often times more than one.
For my life they have set the tone
Just as much as the daily sun.

A friend, a companion, and so much more,
They have always filled my days,
Always waiting for me at the door
Greeting me in many ways.

Each was different, and yet the same,
For they all meant so much to me.
Everyone knew that sound of their name;
They all came running for me to see.

Each one had its special way
Of letting me know that I was theirs,
Laying by my feet at the end of the day
Or blocking my way at the foot of the stairs.

I could never pick who I loved best
For each of them had their special style.
They were all different from the rest
So I could love them each for a while.

Toby

Toby was always the baby of three.
Two older dogs took care of her
But she would learn from what she would see.
As she learned, something strange did occur
For she could do what the others could do.
One was a retriever who loved to run;
The other showed many tricks to you.
Toby thought that looked like fun
She learned to run and chase the ball
Also the tricks of the other one.
We were surprised that she knew it all.
For Toby just always laid in the sun
But then she showed us what she could do.
Just how much she did know.
We were amazed she had learned it too
But then, Toby always wanted to please us so.

Princess

Princess was with me for quite a while;
When I reminisce it makes me smile.
From a tiny homely pup, I watched her grow,
Awkward and clumsy, but never slow.

Soon full grown, what a sight to see,
Sleek and slender and wonderfully free;
Always with me wherever I went,
Our time together was happily spent.

As the years went quietly by
I never thought of the time she would die.
But now I'm thankful for the friendship we shared
All the time that we showed we cared.

Why a Dog

Why would anyone want a dog?
Full of hair and some fleas too,
But just like moss on a log
A dog soon will grow on you.

Chapter
Five

PEOPLE

Happiness

Happiness is a small child's face
As she gives her puppy a warm embrace;
Her bubbly expressions seem to say
We can be happy every day.

Happy Face

A person with a happy face
Always finds an open place
For people are eager to extend their hand
For a cheerful person will understand

A Woman

A woman's mind is a most powerful thing,
With the ability to make a man feel like a king
Or to send him to his greatest despair
With only a cold or icy stare.

Her feelings are always a mystery to all;
Yet, people always come when they hear her call.

Her love can raise up the weakest of men
Leaving them wondering where or when.
Then she leaves them with a smile,
She'll see them again in a while.

Sharing Your Love

Too many days have gone by
Since I last shared your heart.
It seems all I do is cry;
Wondering why our love did part.

Love to Give

A caress, a hug, a gentle smile,
These are things I gladly share.
For the gift of love is always in style
And it will be with you anywhere.

Thoughts of You

I often think about you
Though it's been so many years.
Leaving without a single word,
I have cried so many tears.

I wish that you had told me
Why you had to go.
Instead of just leaving then,
I feel I had a right to know.

Love, hate, jealousy, fear,
All the things that I feel.
Sorrow, sadness, loneliness, too,
None of this seems real.

Year after year continues on
Not knowing of your fate.
I pray that I could finally know;
Before it would be too late.

A Child's Imagination

Where else but in the mind of a child
Could a pile of leaves be perceived
As a fortress of old; a high mountain peak,
A stack of hay, a swimming pool,
An underground tunnel, and a large cave.
What to us is only a pile of leaves,
Can, through a child's imagination, be a wondrous
Playground giving them pleasure for countless hours

Children's Pleasure

It's difficult to understand the simple things that children derive pleasure from. A child can be happy playing with a cardboard box, or a piece of chalk or a pile of leaves or a kite in the breeze.

When is it that they learn to become dissatisfied with everything they have, always striving for more and enjoying it less?

How simple our lives would be. If we too could be like children and once again enjoy the simple pleasures around us.

Time Gone By

A lot of time has gone by
Since that day so long ago;
Yet, at times I still do cry
Wondering why you had to go
For you weren't with me very long.
Yet, my life will never be the same,
Even now my feelings are strong
And you may no longer remember my name.
Yet, I remember your gentle smile,
The tenderness of your touch,
Though you've been gone for a long while,
I still think about you oh so much.

People are Good to Me

People are always good to me
Just the way I'd want them to be.
It seems what I seek is what I find:
Lovely people who are gentle and kind.

What Sets a Writer Apart?

When a writer sets himself apart
Is when his words come from the heart.
For words without feeling only take up space
Until given meaning for others to embrace.

Precious Moments

Precious moments are oh so few
As we travel through our lives.
The times we find ourselves in awe
When a gift from above, a child arrives.

Pink and wrinkled, but alive and well
As she enters her brand new world
How can we ever tell?
As this gift of life becomes unfurled.

Only that she's a precious gift
Given to us all
With our hearts our prayers we lift
To Him who hears our every call.

Babies

To some all babies look the same
But they become uniquely different
When they bear your name

The Lost Child

There's no such thing as a throw away child.
Yet, each passing day it's easy to see
Kids being treated as if defiled,
Put down and degraded for what they try to be.

Yet, there is value to each and every one
Who's given the right to live and breathe.
Their talents and gifts and deeds, they have done
If only we'll look and see and believe.

Yet, so many children are tossed aside,
Never given a single thought.
For those who teach have too much pride
Thinking that they have really taught.

But one special person is always there
For each and every lonely soul.
Seeing their value and showing they care,
They help them find out how to be whole.

Softball

The season's over, done at last;
The lights have all gone out.
It seems to have gone so fast
Though it took a strange and winding route.
Victory was always sweet once more,
But, all the losses hurt again
Even when we were able to score.
At times the other team seemed to win
The players each gave their all,
Working hard every day,
Certainly they should stand proud and tall.
No matter what others may say
Each of them gave their best.
Sometimes they did very well
Working hard to pass the test.
At times they surely could ring the bell.

Thinking of Softball

I can't stop thinking about softball,
The smell of the fresh red rock sand,
The flying dust as I work the field,
The crack of the bat,
The intensity, yet fun of practice,
The joy of watching the girls working
Hard to develop their skills,
The thrill of the games, whether winning or losing,
The sound of the crowd,
The smell of hot dogs and popcorn,
The coaches I know so well,
The umpires who have become my friends.
I hope there will be a time
When I can again be involved
Before I become too old to care.

Chapter Six

FRIENDS

Friends and Gifts

Friends are a gift that we hold dear
They're always around when we need an ear
To vent our anger or share our joy
Our friends will never be cold or coy
With them we needn't put on an act
They accept us as we are, and that's a fact

Friends

Thousands of people all around
But how many friends are to be found?
When wealth and happiness come our way
People come like flowers in May.
But when sorrow and pain leave us in despair,
It is then our true friends are always there.

We All Need a Friend

All of us need a friend
To let us know they really care
And their friendship will never end
No matter what or when or where

I Don't Understand

I just don't understand
Why someone so young has to die.
In my anger, I demand
Give me the answer, tell my why.

He was so young and full of life,
Now we see him lying there.
But we could not see his strife
Nor did we let him know that we care.

As I think of him I feel some fear
Knowing others have problems, too.
Death can always be so near
It could happen to me or you.

We all need now to take a look
At how we treat our family and friends.
For they can't be read like a book
It may take time for their hearts to mend.

None can change yesterday
Or make a difference in the past,
But we can share our life today
Giving a friendship that can really last.

Don't Speak of Love

Don't speak of love, but give it
Don't try to be happy, but do it
Don't preach of faith, but live it
Don't long for success, but make it
Don't cry of sorrow, but share it
Don't shout of joy, but find it
Don't search for peace, but create it
Don't question kindness, but savor it
Don't worry about life, but enjoy it

Am I a Friend

If I had a dime for each time I say
Something kind to a friend
And then a nickel I'd take away
For everything I said to offend

Would I have riches beyond belief
Or find myself deeply in debt
Would I be happy or filled with grief
Satisfied or filled with regret

Yes, I choose to be a friend
Staying with you until the end
Never, ever going away
Caring throughout every day

Friends

If, in a life time, your true friends number three,
you can consider yourself a lucky person

True Friend

A true friend never expects anything in return
His satisfaction comes from the joy he's helped you earn
For his true aim is giving, and showing you the way
And his greatest reward comes from seeing you each day

The Prescription of Friendship

Kindness can cure almost any ill
When used with generosity, it almost always will
For most of our sickness comes from inner strife
Bitterness that can strangle life

When it's treated with the proper dose
Of friendship and love, the cure is then close
For however sick or lonely we are
The key to recovery is never far

So, may God give us strength
To always treat others
With the prescription of friendship
To help them recover

Horrible Harold

Horrible Harold, that can't be his name
Though he never leaves anything quite the same
Wherever he goes, he's easy to spot
If you don't see him, then hear him you aught
For quiet is one thing Harold's never known
Especially when his face is a 'glowin'".
Horrible he's not, some say he's quite dear
Except when he's had too much cheer
We will always think of Harold as gentle and kind
If we should suddenly lose our mind

A Friend

You're a person I'll never forget
Different and apart from others I've met
Filled with insight and deep compassion
Your love for animals knows no ration
Of all the persons I've called a friend
I knew with you I could always depend
To lend a sensitive ear when I was down
Wiping away my silly frown
All through life where ever you go
You brighten the day with your smile's warm glow

A Friend of Mine

A friend of mine stands proud and tall
With a strong body that seldom falters or falls
He's a rough, rugged person who strides through life
Able to weather the storms and strife
Yet, this powerful man has a gentle heart
That puts him in a world apart
For his gentleness and warm affection
Gives his family both love and protection
When God thought of people as generous and kind
Then, He made my friend with this image in mind

Definition of a Friend

How do we define a friend?
A person who's with us until the end?
Or one who will share his innermost feelings
Coming to you when his mind is reeling?
Or is he the one who refuses to leave?
When your world falls apart, and you're left to grieve,
A true friend is really all of these things.
He can be recognized by the love he brings;
He always stands by my side
And he's there for me as my guide.

My Young Friend

I have a friend, so young and wild
Angry from what has come before
For he had been abused as a child
Treated like garbage on the floor

So, it has taken many a year
For him to learn to trust again
Even now it causes him fear
But when that trust does begin

In time he'll find the anger goes
It's not needed to protect him now
From his childhood, he now grows
Rising above it all somehow

Chapter Seven

CELEBRATE

Holidays

Holidays can make you blue
If happiness is what you seek.
For we can't do what others do,
Being sad doesn't mean were weak.

A smile will come when we feel
It's ok to be just me.
It doesn't have to be a big deal
If at times it's hard to see.

For its ok to be sad,
It has nothing to do with the day.
It doesn't mean that we're bad,
Just that we need to find our way.

Valentine's Day

Valentine's Day comes once a year
When we think of love in a special way
Bringing joy to someone dear
Showing we care on the day.

But I've been blessed with a special love
Who brings me cheer all the time.
I can thank my God above
For blessing me daily with love sublime.

Our Flag

Oh, how we love the red white and blue;
That glorious flag waving for me and for you.
It stands for freedom, yet for so much more,
It affects us all to the very core.

The flag stands for everyone who lives in our land,
Enjoying our liberty under its command.
But our freedom has always come with a fee,
Fighting forever for us to remain free.

Many young men have come before
Needing to serve in many a war.
Each has lived their personal drama
Many have returned to tell of their trauma.

But in reality, many have died,
Leaving families, and friends who have cried.
Each of our soldiers served her proud
Fighting for her glory as they have vowed.

All have served their country well
Protecting our freedom where we dwell.
So, when we look at the red white and blue
We know what they have given for me and for you.

Old Glory

We all give praise to old glory
That wonderful flag of ours
As we think about her story
Looking up at her stripes and stars

For so many young men and women have served her
Fighting bravely for her honor and pride
Together working to secure
Remembering all of those who have died

For the mighty old flag has so much meaning to me
And the sacrifices have been so great
But because of them our land is still free
We are able to live at freedom's gate

On Halloween

On a cool autumn day, with the wind blowing strong,
Multi colored leaves continue to fall.
Yet on this day, something seems wrong,
Strange things are happening to us all.

When we look around, it's easy to see
Many eerie creatures on the prowl.
Witches, goblins, and monsters will be,
Wild looking werewolf's, who snarl and growl.

Then we remember it is Halloween.
These weird happenings begin to come clear
All these ghosts and skeletons can be seen,
Only now we don't have to fear.

Once a year comes this day
Where children become their wildest dreams.
From house to house we hear them say
Trick or Treat becomes their themes

Halloween Night

It was a dark and dreary Halloween night
All the monsters were on the move.
We had to feel the sense of fright
Knowing they all were in the groove.

Frankenstein, Dracula, and many more,
Traveling together as if they were one.
We couldn't know what was in store,
Their eerie presence was second to none.

Then we realized that it wasn't real,
All the monsters were not as they appeared,
A sense of relief we now could feel.
Now, we could let go of our fear.

The kids and costumes soon were gone,
They all went home to rest.
The candy and treats will wait for the dawn,
The kids know they have been their very best.

A Christmas Gift

Jesus Christ came to earth
That wonderful Christmas Day.
Nothing's been the same since His birth.
He has guided us to see the way.
Jesus has helped us to believe
In the God who loves us so.
And though in time he had to leave,
His life and love we'll always know.
Jesus gave us another way
To accept God as our own.
Even to this very day
His love for us is shown.
All we ever have to do
To have life forever more,
Is to have faith that is true
That faith will have you at Heaven's door.

Christmas Comes Once a Year

Christmas comes but once a year
Bringing memories of the past,
Warm and tender times are near;
At least, for the moment, they will last.

It's time to remember You my Lord
And all that you have done for me.
A time that family cannot be ignored
As we gather together under the tree.

Yet, it lasts for one short day;
But every year it lets us know
That everything which we pray
Is ours wherever we may go.

Born on Christmas Day

Jesus was born on Christmas day
In a manger so long ago.
Yet, in that stable filled with hay,
God's only son began to grow.

His stay on earth was ever so brief,
But what He did will always be.
Though He suffered much pain and grief,
He died for our sins and made us free.

So, even now as we live today,
We can remember what He has done
Giving us the chance live in His grace
Because of the victory He has won.

Chapter Eight

SOMETHING TO THINK ABOUT

Security

Security is knowing yourself and
being satisfied with your life.

Limitations

I am just beginning to realize some of my
limitations, even though they have always
been abundantly clear to others.

Something New

You will go on to something new
Finding the way to make it through.
Although at times there will be doubt,
You'll have the courage to stick it out.

The Nature of Man

The nature of man is basically good
The problem is he doesn't realize it.

Full of Joy

I feel my life is filled with joy.
For love has always come my way
With all the blessings at my employ
I try to share each happy day.

If love seems a burden, then it is not really love.

Tired

Being sleepy is not so bad;
It's better than being angry or sad.
There's one reward I'd like to reap,
That's to have a little more sleep

If Only

If only I could learn to cry
And let my real feelings go,
Instead of worrying and wondering why
Do I really want to know?

One More Try

When you feel that all is lost
You need to give it one more try.
And though the efforts will surely cost,
You'll know that nothing has passed you by.

If There Were No Problems

If there were no problems, where would we be?
In a shallow world longing to be free?
For troubles give us a tougher mind
If in difficult times, we can always find
Different ways to face life's trials.
Never being afraid to change our styles;
For in order for to be able to survive,
We must learn ways to keep us alive.
Living not in fear, but in grace;
Knowing we can always find our place.

Should I Give it One More Try?

Should I give it one more try
Or has the time come for me to ask why?
Why I've never been given the chance
To show my skills in another branch.

Maybe it's time to realize
I'm just a number in their eyes.
The more I try to prove my desire
The more likely I am to raise their ire.

So, maybe I need to continue on
Doing the best that I can do;
Looking, for a brand new dawn
Then leaving the rest up to You.

Yesteryear

I often think of yesteryear,
The many things that have come before;
All those values that I hold dear:
Love, and knowledge, and so much more.

Now, I look at how much I have grown,
Gaining wealth and power, too.
But so much of what I have shown
Has come from what I learned from you.

So, when I think of days gone by
It always seems to bring a smile.
Then at times, I may even cry
That you were only with me for a while.

So again, I must continue on
Enjoying what is mine today,
Thinking only of what may be,
Following the suns bright ray.

Good Bye Old Friend

Good bye old friend, for you must go,
Though I didn't even know you were here.
It's time that I begin to grow
And that can't happen while you're near.

Although it's easy to cling to you
Because I know you very well.
It's time that to myself I'm true.
What will come only time will tell.

But I know I must be on my way
Seeking now something new.
Ready to start over today;
Doing what I need to do.

Good Bye

Goodbye again, I need to say
Goodbye to what never was
And as I begin to pray
I'll say good bye just because.

A Time to Think

I need a time to think right now
As I find myself confused.
I just don't know when or how
My Lord plans for me to be used.

Something New

You will go on to something new
Finding the way to make it through.
Although at times you're filled with doubt,
You need the courage to stick it out.

Getting Away

I feel a need for rest and peace
Far away from my daily strife.
Where for a while, my worries cease
When again, I let You into my life.

Feeling Lonely

There are times when I feel lonely.
It's usually when I think only
Of my selfish desires and material gain;
Becoming oblivious of the goals that remain:
To share what I have with all those around;
Giving to others is what I have found.
Really living each and every day,
Learning to love along the way.
For when you think of what others need;
It is then that you can plant the seed.
In time, you can watch it grow
Basking together in that warm and special glow.

Life is Like a River

Life is like a river
With its many turns and bends.
Its swift and steady currents,
A mixture that it blends.

It seems to take forever
To travel every mile.
But after every tiring trip
You pause and then you smile.

The currents take you far away;
While the calm pools keep you near.
And though each one has its moments
Both can cause you fear.

When your journey's over
And you finally reach the end,
You look back at it smiling
Like an old and steady friend.

One Life

We have but one life;
May we always live it to the fullest?
Let not one day end in despair
But always in wondrous anticipation
Of the next exciting dawn.
For whatever may happen today
Will help to mold us
Into what we will be tomorrow.
May I always accept what is done
And eagerly continue living
One day at a time,
Always doing the best that I can.

One Day or a Thousand

One day or a thousand,
I really don't care.
I can't foresee the when or where.
All I can do is be me today
Giving of myself in a special way.
I have no control of the time I'll be here
But I will live in faith and not in fear.
For we need not waste a single day
Worrying about what others may say;
Knowing not what is to come
Understanding where our love is from.

But

But is a word that stops us dead.
It always keeps us from moving ahead
Just when were ready to find our way.
But holds us back from starting today,
Finding reasons to always delays
All that needs to be done today.
It's like a cloud hanging over our head
Waiting for something to happen instead;
Knowing the next hammer will fall
Keeps us from giving our all.

Higher and Higher

Higher, higher, and higher still,
Reaching upward towards the sky
On the way you started to groan,
As a matter of fact, so did I.

Climbing can be fearful now;
It can also cause some stress.
But once the fear is mastered somehow,
The pressure suddenly seems to be less.

Fear of Death

I fear not death, but seek instead
more knowledge about living.
For death will come regardless of our feelings,
Without warning and with no concern
for our age or way of living.
So, the only means by which we can combat it
Is by living each day to the fullest.
In many respects, we must always be prepared for death.
Yet, at the same time we should live each day
As if life will never cease.
This will give us the conscience and
integrity to acknowledge
Our mortal selves, and to be prepared
for our eventual end.
While simultaneously having the
faith and peace of mind
To explore all those aspects of living in which we believe.

Why We Fear Death

How sad it is that we often let the fear of death
Prevent us from actually living.
Instead of finding the joy of daily life, and
Exploring the unknown, and challenging ourselves
To find all aspects of living our lives,
We cower and tremble, like leaves about to fall.
When we should be boldly giving
everything in life our all,
Our hopes and dreams are important to us,
Finding their meaning should be our end.
For if our whole life is instead dying,
Which in fact is what fear entails,
We'll never know the beauty of living
When our faith prevails

Need to Let Go

I still need to let go
Of all there is in my past.
For only then will I know
A peaceful time that can last.

A Tear in Your Eyes

Is that a tear in your eye;
That touch of sadness that I can see?
For it's alright for you're to cry
And accept the moment as it must be.

Flying

Rising quickly with a mighty roar
Higher, higher we must go
Until we can begin to soar
Looking down at what's below,

I now feel a certain peace
Replacing that first touch of fear,
Many emotions I now release
As the heavens draw so near.

Floating in and out of the clouds
Now beginning to rise above
Watching that billowing and darkened shroud
That now covers the ground like a glove,

The roar now begins to dim
A certain quiet seems to say
Were on top of earth's rough rim
Now, that is where we want to stay.

A Happy thought

One day I had a happy thought.
I hurried to my friends and I shared it a lot.
It wasn't long till I looked around;
Only happy people were to be found
Its then that we can look back down
To what it was that we had known.
And soon a smile replaces our frown
As we can see how much we've grown.

Learning

We all have so much to learn,
Whether young or very old.
It's not like we each have our own turn
Like an item on auction to be sold.

But learning instead is a gradual thing
Teaching us each and every day.
We are blessed by what learning brings
As we gain in knowledge along the way.

The Emotion of Love

When questioned about the most
important of our emotions
I always respond with the emotion of love and devotion.
Though it may be given or received in various ways,
Its affect can be seen on the dreariest of days.

The warmth of a smile or the touch of a hand
Can kindle the heart, like hot sun on the sand.
If each lonely person had someone to care
Then love would conquer in a manner quite rare.

For other emotions can come and go;
Anger and sadness can make our spirits low.
Picking us up, then letting us down
Causing our smiles to become a frown.

But love again can save the day
Just as a smile can our way pave.
As we let go of our fears and sorrow
The promise of love will fill tomorrow.

Life Is

Life is a strange and yet wonderful phenomenon given to us by our God. One day it may seem peaceful and serene with all of its beauties and natural wonders so clear for us all to see.

The next day it can be so brutal and devastating like a tornado tossing you around and pummeling you with all the ferocity and power seemingly set against you.

Both sides of life are very real and are at times experienced by each of us.

How we handle both the moments of peace and those of chaos help determine the rest of our lives. Although at times we fail to thank God for the serenity and are quick to blame him for the turmoil, He gives these extremes to help toughen us in our faith and to mold us into the people we need to be to serve Him.

Just for Me

Here I am on the other side
Sitting in the waiting room
Feeling lost and short on pride
A prognosticator predicting doom.

How foolish for me to feel this way
For I am here just for me.
It's about time I think of today
Finally, allowing myself to see.

Yet, I still feel full of fear
Afraid to find something new.
But, then I know you'll soon appear
Sharing that you still have fears, too.

When I Feel Low

There are times when I feel low
And it becomes so hard to try.
It's then I wonder which way to go
Finding myself asking why.

But that too can be allowed to pass
If my focus turns to You.
I never have to run out of gas,
When I start each day anew.

For yesterday can be put away
As I can look forward for me and You
Knowing that now is a brand new day
Enjoying it the whole time through.

To Break Away

One step, two steps, three steps four
It's all it will take to get away
Yet, I never get to that door
Where tomorrow could bring a brand new day.

For it seems liked I'm trapped back in time,
Not able to make that final try;
It's like a mountain I cannot climb
The path is removed and I don't know why.

So, then I guess I'll have to stay
For running is not the only choice.
I'm ready then to start this day
Listening to my inner voice.

For I can make it here and now
Trying once more to make it right.
I will make it work somehow
I won't give up without a fight.

Fire's Warm Glow

The fire's warm glow seems to say
Stay by me, and I'll show you the way
For my light will protect you throughout the night
Giving you courage to overcome your fright.
My heat will keep you safe and secure;
Keeping you warm as long as you're here.
The light is bright and continues to glow
Helping each of us to know
That the fire's heat keeps us here,
Warm and safe and feeling so near.
Even when the light begins to subside
We have each other by our side.

Need for the Desire

I have the courage, but where's the desire?
What is it I need to light that fire?
Charging ahead, come what may;
Having the faith to find the way.
Not looking back as I close the door
Anticipating what life has in store.

A Simple Life

Mine is but a simple life.
Simple, yes but free;
Free from worry and from care,
Just as life should be.

Accept Today

So much of our time is spent in expectations of the future over which we have so little control. If only we can focus on what we're doing with our lives now, the future will still ultimately come.

And through our acceptance of today, we will always be able to handle our tomorrow.

Another Day

Another day has come and gone
As we wait for the coming dawn.
Yesterday is in the past,
So enjoy today and make it last.
For each present moment can be the best
So, savor it, then lay it to rest.

Don't Look Back

Don't look back;
For the past is forever gone.

When Will I Live

When will I start to really live
Letting go of my guilt and fear?
Taking the time to really give,
Reaching out to all those near.

Meaning of Freedom

Freedom means so much to me,
Having the choice of what to do.
My dreams are so easy to see
When I know they may come true.

Content to be Me

I am content being me.
I have no need to run and be free.
For freedom is really a state of mind
When we look inside, it's there to find.

It's Been Awhile

It's been a while, I can tell
Since I put my thoughts to rhyme;
But though I stumbled and almost fell
The words came to me just in time.

A Bit of Kindness

A Bit of kindness is all I need
To pick me up when I am low.
For like that tiny mustard seed
It's all I need to make me grow.

Kindness and Love

Kindness and love are truly what matters
When your life seems to be in tatters.
If you can reflect on your life without worry,
Then you'll surely have an understanding jury.
For as God looks down on the path of your days,
He'll see all your kindness and show you His ways.

A Special Wish

A wish, a dream, a fairy tale,
Letting our minds take a trip
Our imagination will not fail
As words and images seem to skip.

Each of us needs some time
Taking a vacation from our routine.
It certainly is not a crime
To create our own peaceful scene.

If only wishes could come true
Everything could be as in our dreams;
How beautiful for me and you
Our wishes as wonderful as it seems.

Chapter Nine

NATURE

Nature's Wonder

Nature's wonders will never cease
Showing her power in splendid release
Flowers bursting from the ground
The colors of spring all around.
Glistening dew to accent the dawn
A beautiful doe, with her fawn
Just as the day finishes the morn
We see a new colt being born
The birds have all begun to sing
Who knows what nature has yet to bring

Beauty All Around

I look at the beauty all around
A budding leaf, a flower in bloom
A carpet of green can also be found
To help us escape from the gloom

The sun chases the clouds of gray
Leaving the sky so blue and clear
Sign that beauty is engulfing our day
Giving us what we hold so dear

Nature's colors are bright and gay
From green and gold to shades of blue
Accented by a sunny day
On display for me and you

Wilderness Test

The wilderness can provide a test
With work and strain around each bend
But it can also bring out your best
And you can see it as your friend

All it takes is some time
A willingness to try something new
The beauty doesn't cost a dime
As you explore it in your canoe

As you finish each grueling mile
With curves and bends along the way
You can't help but start to smile
For all you've done on this day

What is Beauty

What is beauty?
It is the sun glistening
Over the smooth body of water.
It is the lifting of the shadows
To reveal the beauty of the evergreen trees on shore.
It is the craggy mountains with the snow peaks
Somewhat blurred by the morning mist.
What is beauty?
It is displayed in all of its glory
In the northwest country called Washington

Puget Sound

When I look at the tremendous
Blend of mountains and islands
And large expanses of water
Looked down upon by a vast blue sky
There is an occasional silky cloud
High above the water is Mount Rainer
Surrounded by the Cascade and Olympic mountains
Puget Sound is God's beautiful arrangement
Of all of his wonderful gifts of nature
For us all to view and appreciate

It is Ours to See

Beauty is ours for us to see,
All natures gifts and they are free
If only we'll learn to open our eyes
Looking at the beauty of the trees and skies.

Beauty All Around

I look at beauty all around
A budding leaf, a flower in bloom
A carpet of green, can also be found
To help us escape from the gloom

Nature's color so bright and gay
From green and gold to shades of blue
Accented by a sunny day
On display for me and you

The trees are so tall and green
Blooming brightly in the spring
All these things that we have seen
Hearing the songs the birds do sing

Clouds

The billowing clouds over my head
Each one with its different shape
Fluffy and white like a feathered bed
Dressing the sky with a beautiful cape

Rainey Days

Rainey days seem to be here
As storm clouds hover overhead.
But we should not shed a tear
For with the rains our lands are fed.

Brand New Day

I see the light of a brand new day
Giving the signs of breaking dawn
Helping me find strength along my way
Like a doe gently nudging a newborn fawn

Early in the Morning

Early in the morning it is easy to see
All of God's beauty is there for me
The gentle mist falling so light and free
Early in the morning

The grass glistens as the sun begins to rise
Golden rays meeting the blackened skies
Making the colors before our eyes
Early in the morning

Then as the sun makes its way
Giving us the powers of its brightest ray
The view before us begins to change
Early in the morning

Across the Water

The silence of the moment is broken
By the loud hum of the powerful engine
As the ferry glides across
the satiny finish of the Sound

The only other noise is the buzzing of the people
As they view this beauty, and the loud shrill
Shriek of the gulls as they fly curiously by

But even with this intrusion to nature's beauty
Its stillness reaches out and touches me
With a sense of peace and serenity

Certainly God meant for this magnificent place
To be seen by human eyes, but I'm sure his intentions
Are for us to leave this beauty as we have found it
So others too may experience the elegance of His work

The Sun Shines Bright

The sun's never shined brighter than today.
As my lifted spirits began on their way
Into that world that is ever changing
With goals and ideals we're rearranging.
Yet, every step is filled wonder
As we reach for the sky or the sea go under.
For we have learned to find what we seek
Without becoming exhausted or weak.
For only when we find what we need
Will we know how to be happy, indeed.

The Bright Glowing Light

The bright glowing light of the morning sun
Puts God's beautiful language on display
A picture that is second to none
Light of the morning sun

The view is transformed before our eye
For morning is the only special time
For those in doubt, can only ask why
Light of the morning sun

The flowers and trees seem to come alive
As well as the corn and soybeans too
God's creation for man to survive
Light of the morning sun

Dusk

The sun is fading in the West
Beginning its dazzling color display
As it readies for its night of rest
That signifies the end of the day

Night Time

I often look at the evening sky,
So vast and dark yet full of light
The sparkling stars can't deny
Brings a special beauty to the night

Winter's Chill

Winter's chill still is here
Though spring is itching to break through
The morning birds say spring is near
Though the snow still lingers in icy blue

Spring is Near

I heard a bird sing this morn,
Reminding me that spring is near.
Nature's magic will soon be reborn
Wiping away the winter drear.

The butterfly

The beauty of a butterfly
With multi colors on its wings
We watch it as time goes by
All the images it does bring

Sometimes it's near, at others far
Flitting through the air so free
It seemingly freezes us where we are
As it goes its way to where it shall be

Sometimes it reaches way up high
Almost to where it's out of sight
Glimmering and shimmering against the sky
Making its journey by day or night

Then, it suddenly goes away
Leaving us to wonder where it's gone
We really wish that it would stay
And come again by the next dawn

Sweet Summer

Sweet, sweet summer that time of year
When the sky is so bright and clear.
The clouds reflects its shades of blue
That brings its special beauty, too.

The dryness and heat enshroud the day
Bringing the sunshine in a special way.
It's only summer that gives us the sun
And leaves us feeling good when day is done

As the day time slowly fades into night
We still feel the glow of the sun so bright.
When we look up at the twinkling star
We are so happy to be where we are.

The Bumble Bee

Of all the creatures we may see
There's nothing as strange as the bumble bee.
Its body is round and looks like a barrel to me
With wings so small it's really hard to see

Its colors are black and a bright yellow too
Easy to be seen by me and you
This strange and wonderful creature can do
What nature intends for the very few

For it pollinates the flowers and helps them grow
It flits and flies in many ways that it can show
That is how it spends its days
Gathering pollen in the same way

Then it returns to its honey comb
Working hard at its home
Making honey ever so sweet
Just for you and me to eat

The Sky Above

I see the blue sky above
The golden sun shining so bright
Catching the glimpse of a flitting dove
Quickly darting out of sight

Then, I look at the many clouds
Fluffy white and dark and gray
Somewhat like a threatening shroud
Billowing at times throughout the day

Then I see the beautiful lake
With different shades of blue and green
Giving me time to take a break
And look kindly at this wonderful scene

Clouds

Clouds can be most anything
Our fertile mind wants them to be
From a mountain top, to a diamond ring
The shapes are there for us to see

Their beauty at times can't be denied
Reflecting colors of a setting sun
Sharp and distinct before our eyes
With a color display second to none

As the sun sets in the western sky
Giving us a red-orange glow
We know it's time to say good-bye
To nature's wonders we've come to know

Night-time

The night-time air is heavy and wet
With an eerie blend of fog and clouds
That seems like the sky and ground have met
Making dark and menacing shrouds

The gloom seems to cover the day
Changing the mood of all around
It seems as if it's easy to say
Something positive is not to be found

Yet, the night still has its beauty too
For everything seems ever so still
With shadows of gray and silver and blue
Its strange image can free our will

Evening Breeze

The whisper of the evening breeze
Fell lightly on my ears.
Though it's subtle, I do recall
The night transforms us once again.

The sound becomes quite sharp and shrill
As the stars began to glow,
While the dark would seem so still
Waiting for the night-time show.

First the moon begins to shine
Emitting light all around,
Sending the message down the line
Where all who listen hear the sound.

Harvest Moon

Once again I view the harvest moon,
Cornfields almost alive with its light.
My life now seems in tune
Like the moon, it's shining bright.

Colors of Nature

Red, orange, yellow, and gold,
All blended together so well.
What a sight for us to behold
As the day emerges from night's dark shell.

The many colors surround the sun
As it begins its slow bright rise
Showing colors second to none,
Like a large wonderful surprise.

As it continually rises in the sky
Bringing normalcy for the day
Finally answering the question why,
The morning sun has come out to play.

Follow the sun

Our flight tonight gives new meaning
To the phrase as we chase the glow
Of the sun on the clouds
From Minnesota to Washington
It should end in a crescendo of colors and beauty
As we cross the Rockies and the Cascades
As the sun tries vainly to set in front of us
Truly a beautiful site from 39,000 feet above the ground
As we finally begins to descend
Mount Rainer seems close enough to touch
Then through the clouds, everything
becomes a shade of gray
Yet knowing the mountains are all around
As we break through the crowds what a wonderful site
Puget Sound so large and blue
As we touch the ground below
The sun sets, leaving a golden glow

Nature's Colors

Nature's colors are all around
Blue and green and brilliant red
From the sky down to the ground
Not enough can be said

For God's beauty is there for me
If I'll open up my eyes
It's all there for me to see
From roaring ocean to the spacious skies

From the mountain tops to the valley's below
His creation is always there
From the freshwater lakes that thrill us so
To the beautiful palm trees in the dry clear air

Winter is near

The air takes on a crispness
That sends the children inside
A wisp of frost is on the grass
The sky is clear and wide

The weather seems to tell us
That fall is in the air
With all the peaks and valleys
From, cloudy to cold to fair

The leaves are turning color
Orange and yellow and red
The grass is losing its shade of green
The beautiful flowers are now all dead

This certainly tells us that winter is near
With ice and cold and snow
The geese are flying southward
While the trees are looking bare and old

The First Snow

What could be more beautiful?
Than the first snow of the year
That turns the countryside
Into a vivid maze of white so clear

The dirt, the fields, the leaves are buried
The white heavy clouds seem to reach the ground
Making the sky and the earth almost seem married
Winter's wonders are all around

Everything appears so clean and alive
A beautiful scene for all to see
Winter seems to finally arrive
What a place for us to be

Winter's Winds

The winter's winds bring snow and cold,
Chilling the body as their intensity unfolds
Blowing strong and hard, unleashing their fury
Fighting their force makes us weak and weary

Look Outside

I look outside and see the snow
Gently falling from the sky.
It's as if it didn't know
That winter has already passed us by.

Winters cold

The weather outside is bitter cold;
The frosty air makes things glitter like gold.
The beauty though tainted cannot be denied
Helping us see winters powers applied.

Winter's Wonders

Winter's wonders are all around
As we look in amazement at what we have found
The face of the earth has been rearranged
And even God's creatures seem to have changed

The whole winter scene is different and new
It has an effect on all that we do
Although it's quite different from summer or spring
We can accept the changes it brings

For the cover of snow is so fresh and white
Making the sun seem ever so bright
The cold crisp air can give us a chill
But can also be so quiet and still

Chapter
Ten

RAILROAD DAYS

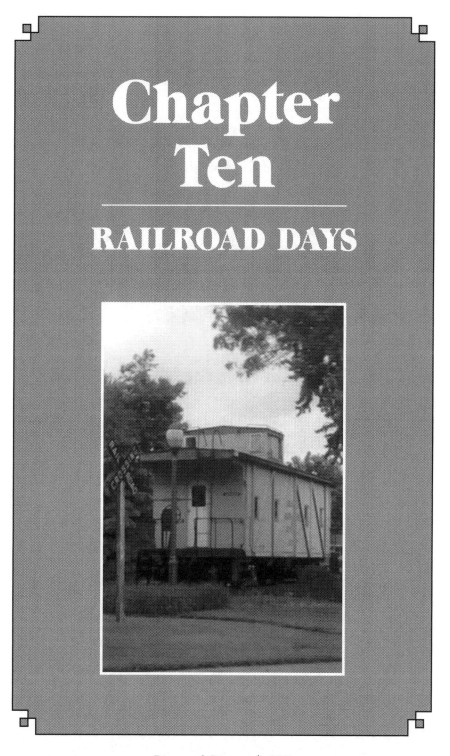

Romance of the Railroad

The romance of the railroad is implanted in my mind
No matter where I go, I am sure that I will find.
I'll still receive a wonderful thrill
Each time I watch a train climbing a hill,
Or see it majestically rounding a curve,
Or crossing a mountain trestle with steady nerves,
Watching it run across the plain,
Whether in the snow or sleet or rain.
How romantic it will always be
In my mind I can always see.

Remembering the Railroad

So many years now have past
Since I left the railroad behind.
But many memories will always last,
Often returning to my mind.

Every time a train goes by
I feel a tug upon my heart.
Is that a tear in my eye?
Has it been that long since we've been apart?

Yes, I'm happy with what I do.
The choice to leave, I know was right.
But the past remains important, too;
It continues to dwell in my minds sight.

A Rail

A rail can be easy to tell
With his special hat that he wears
His coveralls fit him well
The pocket watch show he cares
Knowing when his work will call
Then he'll be ready to do it all

Trains

Each train has its schedule to make
Quickly traveling across the plain
Never stopping by the lake
Ever moving in the tracks straight lane

Once a Rail

Once a rail, always a rail,
At least that is what they say.

A Railroad Man

A railroad man is a different sort
Who comes in all sizes from tall to short.
But one thing that is always the same
His job to him is more that its name.
For being a "rail" is a way of life
Even though it often causes some strife.
For any time of any day,
The job may call you away
Leaving your family and friends behind
For your company loyalty is often blind.

The Railroad Station

The railroad station looks sturdy and fine,
Painted in green or gray or brown or black,
The colors of its railroad line
So close to the track that you must stand back

The Station Agent

The station agent was a sight so rare,
Wearing his visor as he sold tickets there.
Always tending his railroad clock
Like a shepherd watching over his flock.
Deftly using the telegraph key,
Always remembering each destination fee.
Yet, always ready for the train
Carrying baggage even in the rain.
His duties were many and never were done
As he always seemed to be on the run.

Station Masters

The station master was quite a sight
With his uniform so shiny and bright.
Everyone knew he was in charge
Of his railroad depot ever so large.
He sold many tickets there
Remembering each and every fare.
Sending messages with his telegraph key
Proud and confident for all to see.
When the time came for the train to arrive,
There was a certain pleasure he would derive;
Sending people on their way,
So, he could finish the work of today.
Then at night when he closed the depot down,
A happy smile would replace his frown.

The Section

Every rail and tie you see
I put in by myself
With sweat and dirt and my bare hands
So the mighty train could pass.

Telegraph Key

With deft fingers, I'd print the words
That I heard from the telegraph key.
So, I could give orders to the train
Telling them when and where they needed to be.

The Call Clerk

With coffee cup in his hand,
He stares at the names on the call board.
Finding which names are in demand,
Then, to the bunkhouse he runs toward.

Tools of the Trade

The lantern and the pocket watch,
Coveralls and a railroad cap,
After works there's a shot of scotch
Then, to the bunkhouse for a nap.

These were the signs of a railroad crew
At the other end of their run,
Never knowing when there train will be due
But the waiting will not spoil their fun,

But often the beanery would fill their time,
Drinking coffee and spinning tails
After all, a cup was only a dime.
That was important for a lot of rails.

The Watch

With his railroad watch in his hand,
He'll always be able to know the time,
Even when he's having coffee at the Grand
Spending his one and only dime.

Traveling the Rail

Hopping a car to travel for a while
Taking me as far as I want to go
Traveling this way makes me smile
The life of a hobo that I know

The Silver Rail

The glistening of the silver rail
As it goes along its way,
It seems as if it's following the sun,
A strange image we can see today.

The Passenger Train

The glory days of the passenger train are gone;
They will never see another dawn.
With the steam engine proud and tall
Pumping steam and giving its all.

The many people who are bound to miss
For train travel gave a certain amount of bliss.
The peace and serenity was a gift to all
Viewing the mountains so beautiful and tall.

Spending the days so happy and free,
Seeing all there is to see,
Traveling the country at a leisurely pace,
On their journey from place to place.

Hiawatha

I remember well in my childhood years
The shrill, piercing sound that would comfort my ears
The accompanying ringing of the loud elcor bell
Would echo in the valley and certainly tell
That the Olympian Hiawatha was right on time
As it left our valley and began its climb
Over the mountains and toward the sea
Carrying many people that I wished were me

The Iron Horse

The Iron Horse, oh, what a name,
For this remarkable traveling machine.
The way of the horse has lost its fame,
The stage coach was no longer the scene.

For this creature was fed with coal and steam
Blowing smoke into the air,
Man creating a brand new dream
Going where nothing else would dare.

Ten, twenty, thirty, forty and more,
Loudly starting on its way,
It would go faster than man bargained for,
Hundreds of miles in only a day.

All were amazed by the steel's brilliant glow.
The whistle would tell us she was there.
The Elcor bell would let us all know,
That this new train could go anywhere

Relic of the Past

The railroad is a relic of the past,
The glory days that could not last.
When throughout the land people sang the praise
Of the Iron Horse, that cut travel by days.

And the Mighty Steam engine that pulled the train
Through all kinds of weather like snow and rain.
The strong-hearted men who ran the trains
Over the mountains and through the plains

Were certainly made of the strongest stuff,
Rugged and strong with minds that were tough.
We will never ever forget those days
When the mighty railroad earned its praise.

Thinking of Tacoma

I can't stop thinking of Tacoma
Knowing now that I no longer have to go there.
The beauty of Mount Rainer is ever so clear;
The Olympic Mountains across the sound;
The seagulls darting across the water;
The ferries going from island to island.
Then there are my lifelong friends and
The times that we could still have together.
Tacoma itself with hills sharply descending into the port;
The beautiful flowers and green shrubbery;
The smells and sights are all part of it, too.
Just because I no longer have to go
I'd still like to find my way there again.
This time because I want to, not because I have to.

Tacoma Junction

Just a shack by the track
Tacoma Junction was its name
It controlled three railways, a branch line
and two switching yards
It was the only way the trains got through

David Hoye lives in Everly, Iowa with his wife Cheri. They have two children and 6 grandchildren who have played a major role in his writing. His Midwest values and outlook come from his years of living small town Iowa. Dave has published three books of poetry and a non-fiction book about kids. Dave's work in schools combined with his work as a therapist and lay minister has influenced both his writing as well as who he is as a person and his view of the world he lives in.

Other books by David Hoye:

POETRY

Take a Journey on the River of Life
Billowing Clouds, Rugged Rocks and Tall Pines
A Gift of Faith

NON-FICTION

All the Kids on My Block

Printed in the United States
By Bookmasters